PEDIATRIC NURSING

QUESTION BANK

DR. YOGESH KUMAR

Made with ♥ on the Notion Press Platform
www.notionpress.com

The Short Booklet of Pediatric Nursing Question Bank is a valuable resource for nursing students seeking to excel in their studies and prepare for their exams. This Question Booklet is specifically designed to provide nursing students with a comprehensive collection of exercises that cover a wide range of pediatric nursing topics.

The book includes different types of questioning patterns, ensuring that students are well-equipped to answer any type of question they may encounter in their exams. Whether you're a nursing student just starting your journey or an experienced nurse looking to sharpen your skills, the Short Booklet of Pediatric Nursing Question Bank is an excellent resource to help you succeed.

With this Question Booklet, students can easily prepare for their examinations by answering the questions included within the book itself. The questions are carefully crafted to provide a challenging yet engaging learning experience for students. By using this Question Bank, students will be able to enhance their knowledge and understanding of pediatric nursing, making them better prepared for the challenges of their profession.

We hope that this Short Booklet of Pediatric Nursing Question Bank will prove to be a valuable resource for nursing students seeking to improve their skills and knowledge in pediatric nursing. We encourage all students to make use of this book to prepare for their examinations and to continue to learn and grow throughout their careers in nursing.

Contents

About Author

Dr.Yogesh Kumar,Professor, TM College of Nursing,Teerthanker Mahaveer University, Moradabad.

Dr.Yogesh Kumar is a Ph.D, RNRM, and M. Sc. in Pediatric Nursing, currently designated as a Professor at TM College of Nursing, TMU, Moradabad. Has worked for 15 Years at Maharishi Markandeshwar (Deemed to be University). Experienced with 18 years of academic excellence in the field of Nursing Education, Research, Administration, Management, and pediatrics along with special zeal, creativity, and innovations in technology-based education and Nursing care.

I

Multiple Choice Questions (MCQs)

Note: Tick Mark the appropriate answers to the following questions.

1. Signs and symptoms of meningitis in a neonate are all of the following **Except**.

a. Vacant stare
b. Poor cry
c. Neck rigidity
d. Refusal to feed/ sucking

2. The polycythemia in the case of tetralogy of Fallot can best be understood as a compensatory mechanism for-

a. Cardiomegaly
b. Low iron level
c. Low blood pressure
d. Tissue oxygen need

3. Most common site of the congenital megacolon is-

a. Ascending colon
b. Descending colon

c. Recto sigmoid colon
d. Transverse colon

4. Diagnosis of the congenital megacolon is confirmed by-
a. Barium enema
b. Anorectal manometry
c. Rectal biopsy
d. USG

5. The child smiles at the mirror image at the age of-
a. 9 months
b. 6 months
c. 12 months
d. 4 months

6. A 1 liter of W.H.O. ORS provides-
a. 90meq of sodium
b. 110meq of sodium
c. 100meq of sodium
d. 75meq of sodium

7. The most common sign of respiratory distress is-
a. Tachycardia
b. Increased respiratory rate
c. Rapidly declining respiratory rate
d. Rapidly falling heart rate and BP
e. A baby who requires increased heat output

8. The commonest cause of neonatal meningitis is-
a. E. Coli
b. Streptococcus
c. Klebsiella
d. H. Influenza

9. Which type of diet is preferred in case of congenital megacolon-
a. High residue
b. Low residue

c. High protein

d. Low protein

10. In congenital megacolon, the stools are-

a. Hard stool

b. Ribbon-like stool

c. Soft stool

d. Worm-like stool

11. W.H.O ORS solution contains soda bicarbonate-

a. 5g

b. 10g

c. 2.5g

d. 3.5g

12. The complications of oxygen toxicity are

a. Retinal damage

b. G.I tract bleeding

c. Damage to lungs

d. Renal failure

13. The single most important procedure to decrease infection is-

a. Hand washing

b. Gown

c. Masks

d. Gloves

14. A baby turns its head to sound at-

a. 8 weeks

b. 16 weeks

c. 4-6 weeks

d. 12 weeks

15. LBW babies are prone to develop anemia around-

a. 4-6 weeks

b. 6-8 weeks

c. 8-10 weeks

d. 10-12 weeks

16. The crown heel length of premature babies is-
a. Less than 47cm
b. Between 47-49cm
c. Between 49-51cm
17. Top-fed babies have higher-
a. Incidence of sudden infant death
b. Incidence of diarrhea and septicemia
c. IQ on long term follow up
d. Chance of later acidosis
18. Colostrum has-
a. Higher amounts of protein
b. Higher sodium
c. Higher fat
d. Higher carbohydrates
19. In full-term infants, brown fat is about-
a. 1-2% of adipose deposits
b. 4-10% of adipose deposits
c. 10-15% of adipose deposits
d. 16-20% of adipose deposits
20. Which fluid is given in case of severe hypothermia-
a. 60-80ml/kg of 10% dextrose
b. 60-80ml/kg of 5% dextrose
c. 60-80ml/kg of RL
d. 60-80ml/kg of NS
21. What should be the temperature of the NICU?
a. 30 ± 2° C
b. 25 ° C
c. 25 ± 2 ° C
d. 20 ± 2 ° C
22. Why the temperature probe should not be placed on the brown fat area like the neck-
a. Temperature is higher in the brown fat area
b. Temperature is low in the brown fat area

c. It affects the activity of the newborn

d. None of the above

23. Thermo neutrality is-

a. When the air temperature is in the correct range

b. When the infant's body maintains a neutral thermal temperature

c. When both air temperature is in the correct range and the infant's body maintain a neutral thermal temperature

d. None of the above

24. What is the range of axillary temperature in case of cold stress?

a. 36.5 ˚C -37.5 ˚ C

b. 36 ˚ C -36.5 ˚ C

c. Below 36 ˚ C

d. Below 32 ˚ C

25. What is septicemia?

a. Systemic infection of the blood.

b. Respiratory infection

c. Bacterial infection

d. Infection caused by protozoa

26. Treatment of congenital hypertrophic pyloric stenosis is-

a. Pyloromyotomy

b. Colostomy

c. Swenson's procedure

d. Gastrostomy

27. Physiological jaundice occurs-

a. Within 24 hrs.

b. After 24 hrs.

c. After 1 week

d. Within 72 hrs.

28. Milia is a-

a. Pearly white cyst appears on the face of the newborn
b. White cheesy material
c. Bluish discoloration of the back
d. Pinpoint size mark on the abdomen

II

Fill in the Blanks

Note: Fill in the Blanks with the appropriate answers to the following questions/statements.

1. Another name for thalassemia major is ----------------------------.

2. The theory of psychosocial development is given by ----------------------------.

3. The normal mid-upper-arm circumference of children who are under five is about -------------------------cm.

4. --------------------- Type of play is suitable for toddlers.

5. Hydrocephalus is defined as ----------------------------.

6. Wilm's tumor is also known as ---------------------.

7. A signboard mentioning--------------------- should be hanged on the bedside of a child with Wilm's tumor.

8. Duhamel is the surgery done in case of -------------------------------.

9. Loeffler's syndrome occurs due to ---------------------.

10. A sign of meningeal irritation, evidenced by reflex contraction and pain in the hamstring muscle, when attempting to extend the leg after flexing the hip is known as ----------------------.

11. ------------------------------------ Type of leukemia is the most common in children.

12. --------------------------------- are bluish spots seen on the buttocks and trunk of neonates.

13. The birth weight is tripled at the age of ------------------.

14. The term newborn loses ---------------------- of birth weight in the first few days of life.

15. Social smile occurs in an infant at --------------------- years of age.

16. The child sits alone steadily at ------------------------ age.

17. Posterior fontanel close at ------------------------ age.

18. Anterior fontanel close at -------------------------age.

19. Approximately the height of the child at 1 year of age is ------------------- cm.

20. The average head circumference of the baby at birth is -------------------------- cm.

21. Baby can stand alone at the age of ---------------------.

22. The baby can speak two-word syllables like dada at ---------------------- age.

23. The child recognizes strangers at ------------ age.

24. The child smiles indefinitely at --------------age.

25. The child can feed himself a cracker at ----------------- age.

26. The child smiles in response to mother's face at ----------- age.

27. The child indicates when his diaper is wet at -------------age.

28. The child enjoys pulling toy beyond him at ------------- age.

29. The child is toilet trained at night at ----------------- age.

30. The child helps to undress himself at -------------age.

31. Child sits with adequate support and enjoys being propped at -----------------age.

32. The child can put the nipple in and out of his mouth at ---------------- age.

33. Child can hold a rattle for a brief time at -------------------- age.

34. Child holds head erect and steady at -------------------- age.

35. The child can drink from a cup at ------------- age.

36. The child shows imitative expression at ------------ age.

37. The child does not cry when scolded at ---------------- age.

38. The child utters a small throaty sound at ---------------- age.

39. The child learns that by crying he will get attention and crying becomes differentiated at ---------------- age.

40. The child shows emotions like jealousy, affection, and anger at ---------------- age.

41. The child shows hand and eye coordination at ------------------- age.

42. The child knows his name at -------------- age.

43. The birth weight is doubled at the age of ----------------- age.

44. In premature children, gag and cough reflexes are poor, so it can lead to ---------------.

45. The blood volume of a normal newborn is --------------------.

46. Head circumference at birth is -------------------.

47. The normal heart rate and respiratory rate of the newborn is ---------------.

48. Blood sugar levels in hypoglycemia in full-term newborn baby ----------------.

49. The length of a full-term newborn is ------------.

50. Large for date babies will be born to a mother suffering from -------------------.

51. Convulsions in a newborn on the first day of life are due to --------------------.

52. In a neonate ------------------ and ---------------------------- may be the only manifestation of a convulsion.

53. Accidental injection of local anesthetic into the -------------- during the Para cervical nerve block to the mother may cause convulsions.

54. Severe dehydration results in loss of weight up to --------------.

55. Administration of high concentrations of oxygen in premature infants leads to ----------------------------- complication.

III

True or False

Note: Tick Mark the appropriate answers as **True or False** to the following statements/questions.

1. Hyperglycemia may cause convulsions in an infant.
2. Urine output is increased in mild dehydration.
3. Viral pneumonia is more common than bacterial pneumonia.
4. Grey hepatization is characterized by the presence of macrophages in alveolar spaces.
5. Immunization against DPT can prevent pneumonia.
6. The fluid requirement of a newborn is 100ml/day.
7. The crow-heel length of premature babies is 47-49.
8. Neck rigidity and kerning sign are prominent in neonatal meningitis.
9. The febrile seizures are always generalized and never focal.
10. Hyperglycemia may cause convulsions in an infant.
11. Fontanel is sunken in moderate dehydration.
12. Malnourished children are more prone to diarrhea.
13. Perineal anoplasty is done for superalevaroro Anorectal anomalies.

14. The dancing reflex is lost at 3 months of age.

15. Hirschsprung disease is due to the absence of ganglion cells in the bowel.

16. IUGR can occur in the term, preterm, and post-term babies.

17. Low birth weight babies are those whose birth weight ranges from 2000 gm or below.

18. Birth asphyxia is not present in SFD babies.

19. Premature babies constitute 1/3 rd and IUGR babies 2/3 rd of low-birth-weight babies.

20. Multiple births are not an etiology for prematurity.

21. No IgM is present at birth in premature infants.

22. Length is usually not affected in IUGR babies.

23. IUGR infants are underactive, have reduced crying and reflexes are not normal.

24. Hypothermia is not a very serious complication in newborns.

25. The maintenance IV fluid requirement of a neonate is 100ml/kg/day.

26. A preterm baby is any neonate born before 258 days or less irrespective of birth weight.

27. Adequacy of breast milk is best indicated by satisfactory/good weight gain.

28. The fluid requirement for an infant is 50ml/kg of body weight.

IV

Short-Answer Questions

1. Why tonic-clonic convulsions are not seen in infants?

2. List two early signs of neonatal sepsis.

3. What is the amount of fluids given in case of severe dehydration?

4. List two causes of jaundice on the first day of life.

5. Why are fluids administered intravenously in the acute phase of pneumonia?

6. Why is thoracentesis done in case of pneumonia?

7. Why is humidified air administered in case of pneumonia?

8. What is septicemia? How is it related to pneumonia?

9. What is wheezing?

10. What is the treatment of congenital hypertrophic pyloric stenosis?

V

Long-Answer Questions

Fluids and Drugs

1. Write Young's rule for the calculation of pediatric drug dosage.
2. If a pediatric drip set is used, calculate the flow rate for 500 ml of IVF to go in 8 hrs.

Newborn

1. Discuss the characteristics of normal newborns.
2. Discuss the essential newborn care in the area of personal hygiene.
3. Write short notes on neonatal reflexes.
4. Explain the nursing care of newborns at birth in detail.
5. Write a short note on the assessment of newborns.

Low Birth Weight Baby

1. Define LBW baby.
2. What is the nursing management of an LBW baby?
3. What are the physiological problems of small-for-date neonates?

Preterm Newborn

1. What are the physical and neurological characteristics of preterm neonates?
2. What are the physiological problems of preterm newborns?

Nephrotic Syndrome

1. Define Nephrotic syndrome.
2. List the signs and symptoms of Nephrotic syndrome.
3. Explain the pathophysiology of Nephrotic syndrome.
4. Explain the nursing management of the child with Nephrotic syndrome.
5. What type of diet is advised for patients with Nephrotic syndrome?

Perioperative Nursing

1. Write the pre-operative nursing management of children.

Nutrition

1. Discuss the weaning diet.
2. Differentiate the clinical manifestations of Kwashiorkor and marasmus.

3. Write the difference between Kwashiorkor and marasmus.
4. Write down the objectives of the ICDS scheme.
5. Explain the nutritional programs for children in detail.

Pneumonia and Related Problems

1. Define pneumonia.
2. Write the classification of pneumonia.
3. Explain the stages of pneumonia.
4. Describe the causes of pneumonia.
5. Describe the signs and symptoms of pneumonia.
6. Nursing management of the child with bronchopneumonia.
7. Write a short note on bronchitis.
8. Write a short note on bronchiolitis.
9. Write a short note on sinusitis.
10. Explain the pathophysiology and clinical manifestations of bronchial asthma in children.
11. Discuss in detail the nursing management of bronchial asthma.

Hyperthermia and Hypothermia

1. Write the assessment of fever.
2. Write about the stages of hypothermia and their management.

Immunization

1. Write about the immunization schedule.
2. Write a short note on under 5 clinics.
3. Explain various strategies for Polio eradication.

Child Psychiatry

1. Name 5 psychiatry disorders in children.
2. What are the behavioral problems in children?

Meningitis

1. Define meningitis.
2. Describe the pathophysiology of meningitis.
3. List the complications of meningitis.
4. List signs and symptoms of meningitis.
5. List the causes of meningitis.
6. Write the nursing intervention for meningitis.

Eye and ENT

1. Management of foreign bodies in the ear.

Diarrhea and Dehydration

1. Management of dehydration in infants at home.
2. Assessment of a child with dehydration.

Heart Diseases

1. Define congenital heart defects.
2. Write a classification of congenital heart disease.
3. Explain in detail the Tetralogy of Fallot.
4. Define the causes of cardiovascular disorders.
5. Write a short note on tricuspid atresia.
6. Write a short note on PDA.
7. Write a short note on Truncus Arteriosus.

8. Write the pre and post-operative care of a child with Tetralogy of Fallot's.
9. Define VSD.
10. What are the signs and symptoms of VSD?
11. Write the nursing management of VSD.
12. Write about the care of a child with Rheumatic Heart Disease.
13. Write a short note on pulmonary atresia.

Phototherapy, Radiant Warmer, Incubator, Exchange Transfusion

1. Write phototherapy care.
2. Write the nursing care of a newborn undergoing an exchange transfusion.
3. Write the nursing care of a newborn under a radiant warmer.
4. Write the nursing care of a newborn under an incubator

HIV and AIDS

1. Ankit, a 10 yrs. old boy was diagnosed with HIV.
   a. Define HIV.
   b. What are the signs and symptoms of HIV?
   c. Write the nursing management of Ankit.

IMNCI

1. What is IMNCI?
2. What is IMCI?
3. What are the principles of IMNCI?
4. How will you manage a case of diarrhea as per IMNCI protocol?

5. Draw the flowchart diagram for the case management of a child under IMNCI.

Cancer

1. Define leukemia.
2. What are the signs and symptoms of leukemia?
3. Explain the pathophysiology of leukemia.
4. Write the nursing management of a child suffering from leukemia.

Respiratory Distress Syndrome

1. Define RDS.
2. What are the causes and pathophysiology of RDS?
3. Write the nursing management of RDS.

Play Therapy

1. What is play and what is the importance of play in children?

Pain

1. Define pain.
2. List different methods of pain assessment in children.
3. Write pain assessment in children.
4. Explain FLACC scale of pain assessment.

Chromosomal Abnormality

1. What is Down syndrome?

Diabetes Mellitus

1. Write the health education for a diabetic child.

Growth and Development

1. Define growth and development.
2. State the principles of growth and development.
3. What are the factors affecting growth and development?
4. Write the growth and development up to 1 year.
5. Explain the growth and development of toddlers.
6. Explain the theory of cognitive development.
7. Explain the theory of psychosexual development.
8. Explain the theory of psychosocial development.
9. List the role of the pediatric nurse in growth and development.
10. List down the characteristics of growth and development.
11. How knowledge of growth and development helps a pediatric nurse in the OPD.
12. Write the development theory of Freud, Erickson Piaget, and Kohlberg.

Jaundice

1. What is neonatal jaundice?
2. Write the difference between pathological and physiological jaundice.

Neonatal Resuscitation

1. What are the requirements and steps of neonatal resuscitation?

2. Draw the flow diagram representing the sequence of neonatal resuscitation.

Seizure Disorder

1. Write about neonatal seizures.

Spina Bifida

1. What is congenital spina bifida?
2. List different types of spina bifida with diagrams.

Wilms Tumor

1. What is Wilms tumor?
2. Describe the stages of Wilms tumor.
3. Explain the nursing management of a child with Wilms tumor.

Restraints

1. What are restraints?
2. List the principles of restraints.

Cerebral Palsy

1. Define cerebral palsy.
2. What are the types of cerebral palsy?
3. List the causes of cerebral palsy.
4. List the signs and symptoms of cerebral palsy.
5. Write the nursing management of a child with cerebral palsy.

Hydrocephalus

1. Define hydrocephalus.
2. List the types of Hydrocephalus.
3. Write the nursing management of a child with Hydrocephalus.

Tracheo-Esophageal Fistula and Atresia

1. Write a short note on Tracheoesophageal atresia and fistula.

Umblical Hernia And Inguinal Hernia

1. Care of a child with an umbilical hernia.

Cleft-Lip and Palate

1. What is a cleft lip?
2. What is a cleft palate?
3. List down the clinical manifestations of cleft lip and cleft palate.
4. Name the surgical repair done to correct the cleft lip and cleft palate.
5. What are the points to be kept in mind while planning for the pre and post-operative care of a child undergoing surgery for cleft lip and palate?

Hirschsprung's Disease

1. Define Hirschsprung disease.
2. List down the clinical manifestations of Hirschsprung disease.

3. Explain the pathophysiology of Hirschsprung disease.
4. Discuss the pre and post-operative management of Hirschsprung disease.

Thalassemia

1. Define thalassemia.
2. Write about the diagnostic procedures and medical-surgical management of thalassemia.
3. Discuss the nursing care plan of a child with thalassemia.

Acute Renal Failure

1. Write a short note on acute renal failure.
2. Write the nursing management for a child suffering from acute renal failure.

Anorectal Malformation

1. Write a short note on Ano rectal malformations.
2. Write the pre and post-operative nursing management for the child suffering from anorectal malformations.

Miscellaneous

1. Write the management for hypoglycemia a newborn.
2. Write a short note on hypocalcemia in children.
3. What are the rights of children?
4. Write about the concept of a baby-friendly hospital.
5. Describe nursing care for a hospitalized child.
6. Describe the national policy and legislation in relation to child health and welfare.

7. Write the role of a pediatric nurse.
8. Write about the trends in pediatric nursing.
9. Write short notes on mortality and morbidity.
10. Explain the impact of hospitalization on the child and family.
11. Describe various components of the RCH program.
12. Write short notes on enuresis and encopresis.
13. Write a short note on positioning and attachment in breastfeeding.
14. Describe the national health programs for children in India.
15. Describe the various strategies of Polio eradication in detail.
16. Define and give current statistics of

- a. Perinatal mortality rate
- b. NMR
- c. IMR
- d. Under-five mortality rate

1. What are the various physiological handicaps in neonates which make them prone to:

- a. Bleeding tendency
- b. Hypothermia
- c. Fluid and electrolyte imbalance.
- d. Mild regurgitation
- e. Neonatal jaundice

9 798889 354895

Printed by Libri Plureos GmbH in Hamburg,
Germany